Beginning Bagua

a practical guide to training, form and application

by Edward Hines

ISBN10: 1500630551
ISBN13: 9781500630553

DISCLAIMER

The information in this book is meant to supplement, not replace, proper Bagua training. Like any sport involving speed, equipment, balance and environmental factors, Bagua poses some inherent risk. The authors and publisher advise readers to take full responsibility for their safety and know their limits. Before practicing the skills described in this book do not take risks beyond your level of experience, aptitude, training, and comfort level.

Please note that the authors and publisher of this book are not responsible in any manner whatsoever for any injury that may result from practicing the techniques and/or following the instructions given within, since the physical activities described herein may be too strenuous in nature for some readers to engage in safely, it is essential that a physician be consulted prior to training.

Copyright © by Edward Hines 2013

All Rights Reserved. No part of this publication may be reproduced in any form or by any means, including scanning, photocopying, or otherwise without prior written permission of the copyright holder..

For more information about Bagua, essays, techniques, free stuff, seminars and online training visit

www.i-bagua.com

and like our facebook page http://www.facebook.com/pages/I-Bagua/239683522723226

I-BAGUA

Also by Edward Hines

Moving into Stillness – practical qigong meditation

coming soon:

The applied circles of Baguazhang

Baguazhang's key – a practical guide to single palm change

The bullshit free book of badass, beautiful Bagua basics

Contents

Acknowledgements 7
Introduction 8
How to Use this Book 9
    A Note About The Photos 10
An Overview of Gao Style Baguazhang (高式八卦掌) 11
    Xian tien 'Pre-Heaven' or Circular Bagua (先天八卦掌) 11
    Ho tien (後天) 'Post-Heaven' or Linear *Bagua* (八卦) 11
    Tien gan (天干) or Heavenly Stems 12
    Jiben shoufa (基本手法) or Basic Hand Methods 12
    Qigong (氣功) and Neigong (內功) or Breathing and Internal Exercises 13
Partner Exercises 14
    General Groups of Training Methods in *Bagua* 14
    Addiction to Sensation 15
    Violence, Fighting, and Bagua 19
    Ingredients for a Good Fighter 23
    Three Bowls of Rice 25
    Forms and Pieces of Forms 26
    What is qi (氣)? 28
A Special Learning State—Trance and Martial Arts 32
    Simple *Qigong* (氣功) 37
    BASIC HAND METHODS JIBEN SHOUFA (基本手法) ... 42
    Xian tien Bagua (先天八卦掌) 103
    Basic Circle Walking 105
    Single Palm Change 108
    Xian tien shi (先天式)—Pre-Heaven Stance 109

v

Single Palm Change—Dan Huan Zhang (單換掌) 110

Pre-Heaven Palm Changes 1–4 111

Snake Form Smooth Body Palm *she xing xun huan zhang* (蛇形順勢掌) 115

Dragon Shape Piercing Hand Palm *long xing chuan shou zhang* (龍形穿手掌) 138

Returning Body Strike—The Tiger Palm 167
Hwei shen da hu zhang (回身打虎掌) 167

Swallow Form Overturning Body Palm 182
Yan xing gai shou zhang (燕翻蓋手掌) 182

Final words 198
Chinese Glossary 199
About the author 204

Acknowledgements

First, thanks to my teacher, Luo Dexiu (羅德修), who continues to impress me after 18 years, not just with his skill but his perspective as well.

Martial arts don't exist in a vacuum, and I owe a great deal to my classmates, especially Aarvo Tucker, Tim Cartmell, and Marcus Brinkman.

Teachers are not much without students. I'm especially grateful to Nick Cumber and Matt Biss who kept things going after I left London (and because they are not afraid to hit me). Also to everyone else who has paid (or will pay) their dues in sweat, enthusiasm, and thought. Thanks also to Chris Dawson who took the pictures that made it into this book and Jasmina Prill who took the ones that did not.

Tony Felix has helped me get past many martial blocks, coached me through tournaments, and inspired me with his integrity as well as his ability to hit very hard.

Alan Mooney has been an example to me through his hard work, dedication to *Chen Taiji* (陳式 太極拳), and eye for detail.

Thank you to Jenette Antonio for her layout, Jasmine Stephenson for the editing and Jamin Collins for behind the scenes help.

I have also had much patient support from my family, my parents, my daughter Jyoti, and her mother Stephanie.

Introduction

Beginning Bagua is probably the most down to earth, practical book about Bagua currently available.

It is written with the goal of providing concrete, directly useful information on Bagua. This book covers the basics of body use stepping, static posture training, Qigong, key movements, striking and throwing applications, circle walking as well as how Bagua's intellectual framework applies to martial tactics and to general training.

Much of what you will find in this book is useful not just to practitioners of Bagua, but to martial artists in general.

Beginning Bagua is extensively illustrated with photos of both solo movements, basic exercises, palm changes and martial applications.

Bagua is often presented as mysterious, complicated and difficult. It certainly requires study and practice, but this book provides the keys to make sense of the 'abstract' movements, to see the logic behind them and begin to develop useful skills. This book can save you a lot of grief and confusion!

The information itself is presented in a straight forward way, based on direct experience and written with at least occasional humor.

Beginning Bagua is the first book in a series that will look at aspects of Bagua with increasing detail and an emphasis on practicality.

How to Use this Book

In this book, you will find an overview of *Gao style Bagua* (高式八卦掌) along with a number of sample exercises and training methods. There are also several essays on learning, training, and *Bagua* (八卦) in training relating to actual violence.

Ideally, you will use this book to supplement training with an actual teacher. If you do not have a teacher, you need to be especially intelligent and rigorous with yourself to make the most of your practice and avoid tricking yourself in different ways.

Good teachers have a systemic understanding of their art. They have knowledge of the stages that you are likely to go through as you progress. Good teachers also have something else of inestimable value— this is the ability to see you from the outside, both as a biomechanical animal and a human being with particular likes, dislikes, habits, reactions, and ways to perceive the world. They can use this knowledge to tease, humor, frighten, or tempt you into taking the steps you need to progress.

If you are familiar with other styles of *Bagua* (八卦), you will find much that is similar, and also much that may vary from what you have seen before. It is natural, for example, for different styles to emphasize different methods and use overlapping, but not identical, terminology. I trust that you will be able to appreciate what I have written, even if we use the same term for different things, or different terms for the same thing. *Bagua* (八卦) is not homogenized to a single style or set of concepts.

I consider it important to apply intelligence to practice rather than simply follow exercises blindly. Conversely, intellectual understanding is no substitute for practice. Within martial arts, understanding is physical. If you think you understand a concept, yet cannot apply it, then your understanding is lacking. You will need to let go of what you think you know and reapply yourself to physical practice.

A Note About The Photos

We took the majority of the photos on a cold day on Hampstead Heath with Matt Biss and Chris Dawson. We simply ran through the forms/applications as Chris snapped away. As a result, not all the photos are perfectly timed to show the 'peaks' of the movements. I also show various facial expressions. I trust that your imagination can fill in the gaps between photos.

An Overview of Gao Style Baguazhang
(高式八卦掌)

The system of *Bagua* that I learned from Luo Dexiu (羅德修) is divided into several sets of exercises, each emphasizing a separate aspect of the art.

Xian tien 'Pre-Heaven' or Circular Bagua (先天八卦掌)

The *xian tien* (先天) *Gao* style *Bagua* contains circle walking, single palm change, the eight palm changes, and a number of supplementary forms called *wulong bai hui* (烏龍擺尾) (black dragon waves its tail). *Xian tien* contains the fundamentals of strategy and body movement of *Gao* style *Bagua*. The movements tend to be practised in a way that allows the smooth development of power in all directions.

The *xian tien Bagua* (八卦) contains the essence of the art, and its broad, flowing movements have many applications, particularly to throwing techniques. However, the movements are at a level of abstraction that is more concerned with possibilities of movement rather than specific techniques.

Each of the eight palm changes has a function related to health within the model of Chinese medicine. Circle walking is innately meditative, and certain foci of attention can enhance this quality, while others link it more directly to the health building or martial sides of *Bagua* (八卦).

Ho tien (後天) 'Post-Heaven' or Linear *Bagua* (八卦)

The *ho tien* (後天) contains the tactics and application of *Gao* (高義盛) style *Bagua* (八卦). It consists of 64 short sequences of movement that are repeated on the left and right sides, or sometimes linked to create short forms. The aim of each form is to develop smoothness of movement and power for a specific set of applications.

In this branch of *Gao* (高義盛) style *Bagua* (八卦), the *ho tien* (後天) are often practiced in long, extended postures with the aim of strengthening the body and improving balance while making the intention of the movements and the body mechanics clearer to the practitioner.

Tien gan (天干) or Heavenly Stems

Tien gan (天干) are a set of exercises to strengthen the body and develop quality of movement that are rarely found outside of this branch of *Gao* (高義盛) style *Bagua* (八卦). They consist of 10 exercises that are divided into pairs, with the exception of the last exercise, which is divided into 6 variations. The *tien gan* (天干) are typically also practiced in long, extended postures. While it is possible to derive applications from them directly, they are primarily concerned with developing power through different planes of motion.

Jiben shoufa (基本手法) or Basic Hand Methods

The *jiben shoufa* (基本手法) are a set of 8 simple exercises that develop coordination, rhythm, and unity within the body as applied to hand techniques that are found throughout *Gao* (高義盛) style *Bagua* (八卦). Examination of the *jiben shoufa* (基本手法) shows them to be components of xian tien and *ho tien* (後天) palm changes.

Qigong (氣功) and Neigong (內功) or Breathing and Internal Exercises

Various *qigong* exercises are used within *Gao* style *Bagua* to calm the mind, coordinate the body, and develop health. There is also a set of *Neigong* exercises which is more closely related to developing subtle coordination and connection within the body. This is another component of the system that has a significantly meditative quality.

Partner Exercises

General Groups of Training Methods in *Bagua*

You can generally divide *Bagua* into a number of different kinds of training methods.

1. Single palm change and fixed methods

This group of training methods is the most fundamental. The aim is to understand the structure of the body so that it can exert force with little effort. It can include circle walking with the hands in fixed positions, often called *ba mu zhang* (八母掌) (eight mother palms), as well as holding individual steps of single palm change and other forms of *zhan zhuang* (站桩). The body is held with a mix of extension and relaxation that gently stretches the connective tissue of the body, building a sense of unified body movement.

2. Continuous palm

This group includes the continuous palm changes, often called *lao ba zhang* (老八掌) (old eight palms). Here, the aim is to learn to keep the extension and structure of the body while moving fluidly, and focusing the power of the structure in different directions. To achieve this, movements are clear and formal.

In both single palm change and continuous palms, the body leads and the mind follows. You need to clearly observe the sensations and the relations between the individual joints of the body, and help them guide you to efficient, powerful movement.

3. Swimming body palm

In this group of exercises, the movements are more casual and do not necessarily follow a fixed form. Ideally, swimming body palm is practiced once the body is habituated to holding clear structure and maintaining balanced rhythm. In swimming body palm, the movements follow the mind. In some styles, there are specific forms that develop that are used for swimming body palm. However, it can also be considered a free form movement.

4. Special training methods

The previous three groups are related to the general training of the body and the development of smooth, relaxed power. Special training methods are practiced to apply and develop this movement in specific directions, patterns, and uses. Within the *Gao* system, this includes the *ho tien* forms and a variety of partner exercises.

Typically, the first three groups are done one after another, while the fourth is used to refine the application of the first three. It is also helpful to cycle through the different levels, each time adding another layer of body use and understanding.

Addiction to Sensation

A friend described a conversation with his *Taiji* teacher. After several years of practise, he had learned to move in a different way. He really enjoyed the sensations of practising *Taiji*. After one session of intense training and adjustment from his teacher, the familiar and sought-after sensations were no longer there.

He missed the sensation. In fact, you could say that he was addicted to it. He said to his teacher with a slightly confused and questioning quality, "This feels completely . . . different."

His teacher answered, "Good. What you were doing before was not right. If it feels different, then there is at least the possibility you are moving correctly now."

Of all the possibilities that exist of how to move (and how to think), we only use a few at any one time. Many of these will be habitual; that is, you do not need to apply any conscious effort to use them. I am not talking so much about specific movements, like a single palm change, but the components of each movement—the way you lift your arm, or how you brace your body in preparation for incoming force.

Once something has become strongly habitual, it requires a degree of attention simply to be aware of what is happening. The converse of this is when a new organisation of movement is presented, it is easy to assume that it is the same as the habitual one.

We create loops of awareness which run something like this:

"The way to lift an arm feels like x. If it does not feel like x, I shall make adjustments until it does, because if it does not feel like x it is wrong. Sensations that do not feel like x can be ignored; they are not relevant to arm lifting."

Some of the strongest and clearest sensations in movement come from the contraction of muscles. When a muscle contracts, it often gives the agreeable sensation of strength. The contraction may not result in efficient or appropriate movement, but it may begin to feel familiar. The neural pathways that result in the muscle contracting become tied into an increasingly broad range of actions, and so it becomes more familiar.

The above description suggests a positive feedback loop that would eventually result in the muscle being permanently contracted. In fact, to a greater or lesser extent, this can be the case. Most people have chronic tension somewhere in their bodies. I had one teacher say to me, "You are too tense. You are even tense when you sleep." Since I thought of myself as super chilled and laid back, I was originally offended by what he said. Then, on examination, I realised that he was right.

I have lost count of the number of times teachers have said to me, "Relax," while I have thought, "Shut up, I am relaxed . . . or at least I cannot feel where I am tense."

This habitual and inappropriate use can continue to the point where it causes pain and injury over time. I remember once having a slightly injured shoulder. When I moved it in a particular way it would click and ache. Throughout the day, I found myself moving that way just to check if the ache and click were still there. I would roll my shoulder, it would click, and I would say, "Damn, not gone yet." I realised that what I was doing was training myself to move in a way that was clearly not good for my shoulder, but was becoming increasingly habitual.

To successfully learn internal martial arts, you need to reverse this loop that increases habitual tension and reinforces existing patterns. While this applies to learning any new skill, internal martial arts have particularly precise demands on how to reorganise your movement.

The traditional way to do this is to work on relaxation. There are a number of ways to do this. Later in this book, there is an exercise called *fang song* (放鬆功) which you can use to increase your awareness of habitual actions and tension and let go of them.

The key ingredients to let go of these physical habits are soft, slow movement, awareness, and willingness to let go and explore.

In some ways, the less that you are trying to achieve in an exercise, the easier it is to suspend habits. The tension in our bodies is usually attached to a desire to achieve some result. Take away the result and it becomes easier to observe the tension.

People often experience a degree of disorientation or confusion as they let go of old habits and take on new ones. Whether or not this confusion is something that you look forward to will make a difference to your enthusiasm for practise and for learning. Learn to make letting go as pleasant as the new discoveries that it allows.

Luo laoshi often teaches a set of relaxed *qigong* exercises to beginning students. People starting martial arts often want to have results that they associate with the use of inappropriate strength and tension. Basically, they want to feel strong, powerful, and possibly invulnerable. Unnecessary tension allows you to feel your own strength, but at the same time it impedes your ability to apply that strength. The *qigong* exercises do not have any martial intention, so it is easier for people to let go of the habitual tension that comes from striving to feel powerful. Let us revisit my shoulder injury. Once I realised that I was training myself to create a chronic condition, whenever I caught myself searching for the click, I made a game to explore my range of movement as gently as possible without the click. After a while, I forgot all about the click because it was no longer there.

It takes time to return to a good level of relaxation and posture. There is a web of habits to unpick, drop, or dissolve. When you hold chronic tension, it can result in shortened muscles and connective tissues. This restricts your range of movement and distorts the distribution of weight and forces throughout the body. As you relax and let go, it can be uncomfortable, since parts of the body begin to hold their share of your weight that they have not needed to since the tension began.

Since much habitual tension is linked to emotional habits, patterns of thought, and perception, this process of physical relaxation has repercussions that go beyond the physical. It can be accompanied by changes in all areas of life. It is worth remembering that the process is like our very existence and is grounded in the physical.

This process of retraining the body is endless. In practise, you will make breakthroughs, discover new ways to organise your movement, and find new sensations. I trust that some of these will feel extremely pleasant; they will put spring in your step, make you fluid as an eel, solid as a wall, or calm as a still mountain lake.

At some point, you will probably need to let these go and find a new way of organisation. As long as there are people who are capable of doing things that you cannot, in martial or other fields, you will need to continue to let go and do something different to have any chance to duplicate their results.

Violence, Fighting, and Bagua

The public image of internal martial arts is one of flowing, beautiful movements, deep philosophy, and the cultivation of health.

While this image is true, there is also a violent side to these arts. I consider this violent side integral and essential to understand and progress in the arts for a number of reasons.

Martial arts were designed by domesticated primates to get the upper hand in fights with other domesticated primates. Wild primates do not need martial arts; they just bite, rip, and tear in a simple and effective way. If you don't believe me, go and annoy a chimpanzee.

So *Bagua* and other martial arts are a bit like taking a scientific approach to being a Chimpanzee-with or without weapons!

Actually, I stress our animal nature because when we try and ignore it, it just comes in again through the back door. I think it is wiser to consciously embrace and integrate our animal nature so that it can better support our uniquely human characteristics.

Fighting and play fighting is something most mammals engage in. Little boys, puppies, kittens, and baboons all wrestle. It is a very effective way to develop the body, coordination, and reflexes.

When we consciously engage in martial arts, we gain the primordial physical benefits that such work entails.

We also reacquaint ourselves with our animal nature, which gives us greater choices when it arises in us and threatens to sweep away our civilized habits.

I once read about a martial artist who worked the doors of rough nightclubs because he wanted to live "in real life." He said that he felt sorry for those people who think that life is nice, or safe, or comfortable. For him, life was hard and brutal. Those people who enjoyed gentle lives were just delaying the inevitable cruel awakening.

In many ways, of course, he is right. No amount of comfort can save us from inevitable death, or the death of the people we care for.

Under certain circumstances, human beings behave abominably. There are enough tales of genocide from recent times to have no doubt about that.

It is equally true that under certain circumstances people behave with the greatest nobility and generosity.

Given that both are true, which would you prefer? The question is then, how can you create the circumstances, both internally and externally, for the situations that you prefer?

When you spar and practise dangerous techniques, you develop an awareness of the fragility of the human body. You receive the techniques with your own body and work with the bodies generously provided by your classmates. You get to feel very mortal. I find that this helps develop compassion and the ability to accept what is.

Sometimes things go wrong. Someone gets hurt, and their temper rises (nothing like getting smacked in the nose for this). In that moment, they have a choice: to lose themselves in animal rage or keep an awareness that is larger than the emotion.

Fighting technique is also very earthy and very grounding, provided the feedback is honest. Where the syllabus involves meditation and practises that can take people deeply into their internal subjective experience, partner work provides a balance rooted in interpersonal experience.

While you meditate, you may *feel* dragon power coursing through your meridians. If you unleash your *qi* on your partner and they do not notice, then you have had a lesson in the boundaries between metaphor, sensation, and the essentially Newtonian world we interact in.

In my life, I'm fortunate enough to see fairly little violence outside of class. When it does happen, however, I am better able to deal with it.

Violence is just another kind of communication, another language that I am able to speak. Punches and kicks mean, "Look at me, I am important, acknowledge my worth."

When the syntax in a dialogue consists of blows, intellectual ideas and the words that convey them are unable to engage actively. The communication is primarily somatic, from before the pushing and shoving starts until the blows start to fall. An intellectual argument in a fight communicates as effectively as a letter for your pet dog.

If someone insults me verbally, I may not like it, but I can deal with it. I have a number of mental strategies that provide me with choices as to how I can respond.

Equally, if someone hits me, I have a choice. I can walk away or engage. I can engage with the intention of escape, or to render my attacker harmless. I do not need to be traumatized or enraged any more so than by the verbal insult. Chances are, I've been hit harder in class by people who I like. Why let myself get upset by a flailing drunk?

Of course, there are limits to this. If I was beaten to a pulp, I might probably be both traumatized and enraged. There are many, many people out there more competent at violence than me.

For many of them, violence is not a form of communication, but a tool. I have very little experience of targeted, professional violence, and consider it largely beyond the limits of what I feel competent to talk about.

The important point is that in emotionally-fuelled conflict, I have a choice, both physically and mentally.

When people engage in martial arts without sparring and contact, they often fuel their fantasies of power. At the same time, they are unsure of their physical capabilities. This often surfaces as passive aggression, such as sniping at other styles. This results in a sense of superiority many 'internal' martial artists feel towards boxers of 'external' styles.

As a result, I advocate sparring practise for any martial artist who wants to remain grounded. However, there is a shadow side to this. Martial artists who test and develop their fighting skills often go through a period of pride. Some learn to suppress their capacity to feel for others to better inflict violence on them. Their training may be driven by fear of being beaten rather than the pleasure of developing their minds in movement.

I think these shadows are especially prevalent when a teacher has a cruel streak, or where hierarchies exist based on seniority. For example, "You cannot hit/throw/beat me because I've been training here longer than you. But I have the right to hit you . . . "

In martial arts, the healthy attitude is to be concerned with your own skill and control while engaging with others so as to learn from them. Direct comparison often leads to insecurity on one side, feelings of grandeur on the other, and often both. "I'm better than Joe, but Mike can still beat me."

I once admitted to a musician that in social situations I sometimes had a sense of insecurity. During these times, I might tell myself, "He may be more handsome/charming/rich than me, but I could probably beat the shit out of him." The musician laughed and said, "Yes, I do the same, except I say that I can play the trombone better!"

The question is not, "Am I tougher than him?" This kind of comparison rarely leads to pleasure. A better question is, "How can I use these skills to the benefit of everyone around me?"

Ingredients for a Good Fighter

As you learn more about *Bagua*, you will start to come across stories of incredible martial artists who defeat hordes of opponents, or perform incredible feats of power, agility, and precision. There is a reputation within *Bagua* that it trains ultimate fighting skill—float like a butterfly and slap like a grizzly bear to paraphrase a boxing legend.

What has happened over a number of generations is that people gravitate to the aspects of the arts that suit them best, or threaten them least. Typically, these are the graceful, flowing, meditative movements and the stories. The first give pleasant sensations and an overall feeling of well being. The latter give a sense of direction, context, and meaning. However, the combination of these two will not create the ultimate fighter.
If you look at the greatest fighters, they have one thing in common. It is not the style of the art they practiced, if they practiced any style at all. It is their capability for violence and their willingness to fight and hurt people. (I realize that *Taiji* idealists will say that Yang Luchan (楊露禪) took on many challengers and defeated them without injuring them. I say that they need to check their sources.)

Since these fighters were willing to fight and to risk serious injury to themselves and their opponents, they got more practice. They understood what they could and could not do in a violent situation. They developed reputations that attracted challenges from skilled and unskilled opponents, and thus increased their skill.

This willingness to fight and hurt people will not come from your slow, soft practice, or even your hard, vigorous practice. It may come either from having no choice, from habit, or from not caring. For some, it comes from a hunger to prove themselves in this way, to meet a self image of a tough person. For others, the willingness to hurt may come from an underlying fear of being defeated.

Violence is attractive; it holds a fascination. Modern media is filled with violence, some realistic and some cartoon like. The world is also full of violence. There are countries at war, dangerous neighborhoods, and little pockets of hell that flare up and die away with the tempers of ordinarily peaceful people.

Violence is fascinating because understanding it offers survival value. Violence may be unlikely in your current situation, but is certainly possible, and the consequences can be terrible. One violent incident can change or end your life and the ability to pass on your genes. So, from an evolutionary point of view, it makes sense to swiftly learn as much as possible from violent incidents.

We learn fastest in a state of curiosity and absorbed fascination, and so from a learning perspective it is adaptive for us to be fascinated by violence.

Since it confers survival value, the understanding of violence is often used in human mating displays. You can see this very easily on a Saturday night at a nightclub near you.

The greatest fighters also trained like demons. Training for half an hour to two hours a day is not a lot. Modern combat athletes and ancient martial artists alike fill their waking hours with physical training and the study of tactics, strategy, physiology, and other related subjects. At night, they dream of martial arts and fighting.

Bagua and all internal martial arts are hard work. The soft and sensitive practice is both the icing on the cake and the foundation. You need to change how you move, to let go of old habits and put new ones in their place. The daily hours of some *Bagua* circle walking is to develop new ways to move and to refine existing good habits. It is not a substitute for actual partner practise, sparring, and fighting. However, solo practice will help you make the most of the partner practice that you do.

Generally speaking, martial arts were developed for people who were already capable of violence to make them both more efficient and less random or more controlled in their application of it.

These days, the students of internal martial arts are typically people who are not used to violence, and are generally unwilling to risk injury to themselves or to hurt other people. This is a good thing, since actual violence is dangerous and dehumanizing. However, it does tend to encourage people to drift in the direction of fantasy capacities supported by ancient stories and the interesting sensations that come from training.

It is better to recognize and accept that even if you practice an art with an amazing reputation, if you are not inclined towards violence, you will probably never become a martial legend.

It is good to simply enjoy what you learn, to take yourself out of your comfort zone as you train, and apply what you learn to minimize the risk in potentially dangerous situations.

If, on the other hand, you are already a violent person and you find yourself attracted to *Bagua* (八卦), then be patient with your classmates and teachers who may know less about hurting people than you do. Use the art as a way to refine your movement and increase the amount of choice you have in different situations, whether before or after violence has begun.

If your goal is to become the ultimate fighter, then you may find ideas and skills within *Bagua* (八卦) that will help you along the way.

For most of us, it is good to recognize exactly how far we are willing to go along the path of martial mastery. We can enjoy the stories of wonderful ancient masters as entertainment with occasional educational value, rather than confuse them with the important goals in our lives.

Three Bowls of Rice

Internal martial arts are filled with fascinating details of body use, which lie upon an intricate tapestry of stories, legends, and myths. Only high level teachers can impart the skills and secret training methods that make the amazing feats described in stories possible. These secrets are sought after avidly by students and marketed enthusiastically by teachers.

When I started with Luo laoshi, I was amazed by how down to earth his training methods were and how they improved my skill. But I was still greedy for secrets. In those days, Luo laoshi would often use this analogy.

> *"Imagine being hungry, really hungry. To fill your belly, you need to eat three bowls of rice. You need to eat the first bowl, the second bowl, then the third bowl. You cannot go straight to the third bowl and just eat that. Students who come to internal martial arts looking for 'secret' or 'advanced' techniques are like people who just want to eat the third bowl of rice."*

I like to take the analogy a culinary step further. I think of the advanced techniques as a sweet "dessert." If all you eat is dessert, then you run the risk of being both malnourished and overweight, not to mention losing your teeth.

If you want to develop skill in *Bagua*, you need to work on simple basics, simple basics, and simple basics. If you ever get beyond these (and if you do them well they will provide plenty of benefits), then you can think about doing tricky advanced methods.

Bon appétit!

Forms and Pieces of Forms

The majority of people who start internal martial arts, and Chinese martial arts in general, spend a great deal of time learning forms.

There is even a belief that the practice of forms somehow magically confers fighting ability.

However, the reason most people teach and learn forms is because they are easy. Forms have a variety of movements, which make them more interesting than single movements. They can include the same movements in different combinations, which means you get something new, while at the same time having the comforting aspect of doing something familiar.

You can feed forms to students for years, with the promise of the next even more advanced/magical form just around the corner...

But forms are not where the skill lies. The skill comes from discovering the fundamentals of body use and working them through individual movements. Some of these movements may be in the forms, others may be found in *qigong* sets and static postures. Fighting skill comes from combining these insights and ways of moving with fighting practice.

Forms act as either entertainment or a smokescreen to hide the real skill, or a physical mnemonic for people who have already developed their fundamentals.

Gao style *Bagua* has, from one perspective, a great number of forms—8 circular palm changes and 64 straight line palm changes. It can be very easy to get into the form trap, learning and remembering so many forms.

From another perspective, *Gao* style forms tend to be very short. They each take just a few seconds to do, and some are so short that they can almost be considered individual movement practise.

When training, rather than trying to practice lots of forms linked together, it is usually better just to concentrate on one.

In fact, you can even just take a piece of a form and repeat that again and again.

If you do this, you can go deeper into each movement, provided you maintain your attention on the movements. Then it is relatively easy to generalize the insights and understandings you have gained to other movements.

What is qi (氣)?

This is a question which is often asked by the aspiring martial artist who searches for a neat, simple answer. Our Western materialist minds are often primed to expect a material answer, that *qi* is a particular energy, or perhaps a mysterious fluid.

However, as soon as you start to look for an answer as discrete as the ones above, you soon discover that the method of looking at the question will actually hinder your ability to find a satisfactory or useful answer.

In Chinese culture, *qi* refers to many different things in different contexts. For example:

Qi eo (氣油) is petroleum (literally qi oil), tien qi (天氣) is weather (literally heaven or sky qi), sheng qi (生氣) is angry.

You cannot reduce *qi* to some convenient measurable fluid. It is much more like a verb or adverb referring to processes of connection and flow than a noun.

Within Chinese medicine, *qi* refers to the flow and connection between organs of the body. The *qi* of martial arts, though also within the body, is different, but related, because the function is different.

As I attempt to explain this, I will refer to Western concepts and structures. While I am aware that this can be a little reductionist, it seems preferable to me.

The alternative, which is to try and explain without clear points of reference—that is, points from an unfamiliar culture—leaves people floating. As they float, they gravitate towards what is dominant in their imagination, which is why there are so many martial *qi* fantasists out there.

So let's look at *qi* in the context of martial arts, or the skill to be able to injure people without them being able to injure you. Let's also start with the ideas of another Western martial artist.

Moshe Feldenkrais was an engineer and a student of Judo's founder, Jigoro Kano (嘉納治五郎). Feldenkrais was also the originator of a sophisticated form of body work, and he had his ideas about *qi*.

His ideas were purely pragmatic. In his opinion, you had *qi* if you could do something that demonstrated *qi*. His frame of reference was the high level judokas who were able to throw people effortlessly 'because of *qi* '. For him, this was a kind of neuromuscular organisation (a skill) that allowed them to maintain a type of relationship with someone else who had a different kind of neuromuscular organisation (less skill). Up to a point, I agree with Moshe—coordination and balance are a component of *qi* in martial arts.

I believe that there is more to *qi* than coordination, balance, and other aspects of neuromuscular organization. These other aspects can be seen in different aspects of martial arts. However, either because they were not present in the Judo he studied, or because they were hidden from him, these were not evident to Feldenkrais.

Let's consider some of these. As well as the ability to hit and throw people, *qi* is also referred to in martial arts with respect to being able to absorb shocks or prevent cutting. Martial artists who have developed their *qi* are said to have bones that become like steel.

People who practice internal martial arts often have a rounded form in terms of their body and limbs. This can extend to their face (which as a result looks younger) and fingers, which are somewhat "puffy."

In Chinese martial arts, people would grasp another person's wrist as a test of *qi*. It's similar to taking a pulse, but not identical.

What are the common points between these types of phenomena? Let's start with the wrist. As you touch it, you feel the development of the tendons, which are connective tissue. Remember that *qi* is related to flow and connection.

The roundness comes from the working of connective tissue below and in the skin. As this builds up, the skin naturally gets tougher. The same process of working the connective tissue internally accounts for the body's ability to absorb blows.

The hands and feet are like the tuning knobs on a stringed musical instrument. They are at the extremities. The sound is developed in the body of the instrument, but this can only happen if the strings (tendons/meridians) are held at the right level of tension. Working this way with the hands leads to their puffiness.

So there is a training of skills and the specific coordination, as Feldenkrais suggested. There is also a change in the composition and structure of the body. These developments reinforce each other. As the body changes, it becomes more natural to apply the kind of coordination that stimulates the change.

The structures of connective tissue that are trained in these arts are normally outside of conscious awareness. To access and train them requires patience, concentration, and tricks.
The patience and concentration explain the meditative and trance-like aspects of *qigong* (氣功). The tricks are the details of posture, like the use of the hands as tuning knobs. Twisting the body, concentration on various points, different ways of breathing, the use of the voice, and various visualizations are also tricks. Different martial arts styles tend to emphasize different "tricks".

Just because I refer to these details as tricks does not mean they do not require lots of work to apply.

The concentration required for the body control that is important in *qigong* is similar to that required by meditation, so there is a lot of crossover in the effects.

The connective tissue that is being worked follows functional lines along the body that relate loosely to the meridians of Chinese medicine. The connective tissue wraps around the bone as the periosteum, and effects bone resilience, density, and healing.

Deeper into the body, the connective tissue encompasses the internal organs. This includes the endocrine system right up to the pituitary and pineal glands and other parts of the brain that regulate much of metabolism. These have been posited as being responsible for spiritual experiences.

So where I started almost apologizing for a reductionist approach to *qi*, I have ended with a system that is intricate and encompasses mental, emotional, hormonal, muscular, connective tissue, and nervous systems of the body. It includes pretty much everything really, which is not so surprising. The body is one whole, and attempts to divide it into different parts are mental constructs.

This is still an overtly materialist explanation of *qi*. It does not encompass the actual experience of working in this way. It is also focused on the developmental *qi* in martial arts and does not consider the wider context. This explanation is similar to attempts to separate out components of the human body. These attempts ignore the whole, and while useful in a narrow sense, they are ultimately misleading. Just as separating a martial art(ist) from the broader context of meaning and wider life is also ultimately blinkered.

A Special Learning State—Trance and Martial Arts

Milton Erickson, one of the most influential hypnotists of the 20th century described, if not defined, trance as a "special learning state". His student, Stephen Gilligan, talks about trance as a natural state that happens whenever our identity is threatened, and at times of our life when our identity undergoes a natural change. A quality trance, in his opinion, is one where the intellect is dropped down into the body, the body connects to the "field," and the person remains present in some way. Stephen Gilligan also describes trance as the ability to think without physical tension, and makes distinctions between ordinary intellectual logic and trance logic.

Normal intellectual logic is linear and follows linear rules. Normal logic follows a designated cause and effect, meanings are fixed, and things cannot be their opposite. Normal logic provides an either/or way to think.

Trance logic is the logic of dreams. You can go from anywhere to anywhere, meaning is fluid, or suspended, something can be its own opposite, and contradictions can sit comfortably together. Trance logic is a both/and way to experience.

If you look at the spiritual literature that make up part of the cultural landscape in which internal arts evolved, you will find plenty of references to the virtue of not knowing, the limits of knowledge, and some lovely descriptions of trance logic.

Within the martial arts themselves, you can find references to putting attention down into the lower abdomen and relaxing the body—both are techniques, or components of techniques, for inducing trance. The founders of many martial arts were also known for their eccentric ways and their ability to think outside the normal intellectual and social rules of the time.

The intellect alone is pretty limited when it comes to martial arts, which does not stop many people from theorizing endlessly about the way martial arts should be. When people are training well or fighting, I've never known them to be intellectualizing. On the other hand, there is often a state of detached observation mixed with a sense of total involvement; both/and rather than either/or.

In Gilligan's model, he also says that trance is a state we naturally go into to reorganize our identities, or our sense of who we are. It allows us to escape the social and intellectual strictures which contain what we expect of ourselves, how we should behave, and what we can do or not do. These kinds of trances are especially important at turning points in our lives, and when we are faced with various kinds of trauma, loss, and change.

Within the slow, rhythmic practises of internal martial arts, there is plenty of scope for depth of trance. What purpose do these trances serve?

Purely in the context of martial arts, they allow a suspension of intellectual activity and the non-stop labelling of right or wrong and good or bad that can stop us from observing what actually happens. When this is suspended, the body, which knows itself much better than our thinking mind knows it, can then begin to do things in new ways. It is the strait jacket of "knowing" what's "right" that is one of the greatest obstacles to learning.

So, from a Western point of view, you can look at some of the mental focussing techniques as a way to improve the learning process, both in being open to ways to improve your use of your body and to develop states of mind that are martially useful.

Of course, if you spend a lot of time going into deep trances, you'll probably have some pretty strange experiences sooner or later—strange sensations when you practise, intuitions, perhaps even visions. It's the nature of trance experiences that cause the boundaries between the imagination and "reality" to blur or disappear altogether.

Most people take these experiences in their stride. Some people, on the other hand, do not. Perhaps due to emotional imbalance, difficult circumstances in external reality, or lack of maturity, preparation, or context, they take the strange experiences either as the goal of practise, or they take them literally. These people often turn their martial arts into bizarre religions and spend their training time chasing the dragons of their imagination, and then construct elaborate intellectual cages to contain them.

Unfortunately, this doesn't necessarily make them happier, healthier, or better at martial arts. I think much of the advice to "find guidance from a good teacher" is an attempt to stop people going off on these kinds of trips.

Outside of the martial arts, the ability to go into this kind of healthy trance can be very helpful too. It allows us to hold contradictions that we face in daily life without going insane, and to remain fluid in the face of seemingly solid problems.

As an example, let's take a situation filled with strong emotions, anger perhaps, or sadness. Combine this with the ability to remain physically present, to keep part of the attention in the body, typically low in the abdomen in martial practises. If you do this, it fosters an appreciation that while there are things labelled as bad (the emotions), at the same time there's something else (the calmness of the abdominal attention). Without this physical presence, it is easy to get entirely caught up in the emotions and the thoughts about them. These thoughts tend to run in loops and stories that justify the negative emotion and lead to automatic reactions that often maintain the conditions that the emotions are linked to. With physical presence, it becomes easier to detach from the automatic thoughts and emotions and to be aware of more possibilities, along with the possibility of choosing wisely between them (or not!).

An internal martial arts practise that has scope to develop trance is also useful as training to enter states where we can learn from what life gives us. These states can help us mature in the face of the universals of age, love, and loss, rather than having to resist them because they affront some aspect of a rigid identity.

So if these states are so useful, how do we access them? The first answer is, of course, practice!

Luo laoshi emphasises a few very simple ways to develop these states. Many of the methods are common to other martial arts styles, and once you've caught the concept, you'll see it repeated in all sorts of places.

The main idea is to harmonise the mind and emotions at the start of practise. The way Luo recommends this is through slow, repetitive movement.

Slow, because fast movement tends to excite the emotions, and because slow movement allows the attention to go deeper into the body. It's possible to substitute no movement for slow movement, but the mind tends to calm more easily when it's given a simple repetitive task like repeating a gesture.

One of the vehicles Luo uses for this is *ba duan jin* (八段锦 eight pieces of brocade), because it's so simple, and when practising, people don't get caught up in all the emotions involved in learning "super deadly" martial arts.

Another important idea is to create a context where there isn't pressure to perform in the practise. In circle walking, Luo suggests simply walking a certain number of steps. It does not matter if you do it well, just walk the steps. This releases the mind from the need to perform, and allows it to pay attention to what's happening. After a period of walking, the mind and body tend to settle naturally, and then the walking can absorb your attention deeply.

Parallel to this attitude of not really caring what's happening in the body, you can develop an equally abstracted attitude towards your thoughts. The eyes look, but don't really see. The thoughts come and go without the emotions getting aroused, and if the emotions start to move, you can observe them with vague and benign curiosity.

While doing this simple repetitive task, you can choose one or two specifics to focus on. For instance, you could choose an overall relaxation of the body, or some specific part of the body, such as how the hips, torso, and spine connect, the footwork, or the alignment of the arms. With time and a deepening of attention, you get to the state where "the body teaches you". It ceases to be necessary to try and fix the posture to some rules in a book or rely on the corrections of a teacher, but it becomes evident what needs to happen.

Over a longer time scale, the same applies. You do not have to approach practise with the idea of attaining some goal by a fixed date. Happily, by releasing the pressure and the intellectual stricture in training, progress is quite likely to be faster. It's also likely to be non linear; rather than improving a little bit day by day for stretches of practice, it seems like there's no improvement, then suddenly there's a jump in ability or quality.

Once you've found a way into it this state, it gets easier to access. Part of the key to making the access easier is to finish practice well. Rather than stopping practice and running off to go shopping, spend a little more time in stillness, with the attention absorbed internally, before making the transition back to ordinary life and consciousness.

This is something that often becomes ritualized in martial arts. Lifting the hands up and out from the body, then down along the centre line are examples of this. A movement common to the end (and start) of many forms is used for this purpose. While this is one function of the opening or closing movement, it is by no means the only one.
Along with the movement, there is also the idea of gathering the energy back to the *dan-tien* (丹田), which refers to the placement of attention. It includes the idea of stilling the emotions that may have become aroused and realigning parts of the body that may have become disturbed or tense during practice. This way, the body is well prepared to continue daily life, and a good state is associated with the movement for the beginning of the next practice.

Of course, martial arts aren't only simple movements, interesting states, and comfortingly blurry statements like "your body teaches you". There are complex movements too, though the interesting states can help you appreciate their relation to the simple ones. There is also rigour, conditioning, and the test of whether a movement can actually work.

Within the context of special learning states, there is more in terms of possibility and depth than I have described above. What I hope that this article has done is to help you appreciate the value in the ritual that goes with martial arts. This way, rather than looking at it with distrust, confusion, or religious incomprehension, you can approach it as a tool that can aid your development as a martial artist and as a human being.

Simple *Qigong* (氣功)

To develop active control of your body, it is very helpful to have a method of increasing your body awareness and mental clarity. Physical tension in the body excites emotions and mental activity. It also makes you less sensitive to the forces that act on your body from the inside or the outside. Reducing the forces on the inside is vital to increasing efficiency of movement, and sensitivity to external forces is vital in martial arts.

Fang song gong (放鬆功) is a generic name for relaxation exercises—it literally means relaxed skill. There are a variety of different approaches that I have learned to *fang song gong* (放鬆功). The following is a version that Luo laoshi (羅老師) teaches. It has a thorough structured quality that I like, and it ties in to some of the other *Neigong* (內功) and meditation exercises that he teaches.

Luo laoshi (羅老師) likens doing these exercises to resetting a machine so that it can run more smoothly. Just before I started writing this section, I restarted my computer as it was beginning to act up. The similar practise of *fang song* (放鬆功) helps keep the mind clear and the body sensitive. It facilitates letting go of the thoughts and tensions that take up increasing amounts of mental space over time.

Fang song (放鬆功) is similar to *yoga nidra* (yogic sleep); however, unlike *yoga nidra,* which is practised lying down, *fang song* (放鬆功) is practised standing up. While it is possible to enter a deeper state of relaxation while lying down, since we are martial artists, we want to develop the capacity to relax while active and vertical. It is also easier to remain awake while standing. *Yogic sleep* can often transition into simple *sleep.*

1. Stand upright, feet hip to shoulder width apart. Imagine your spine being pulled upward by a point at the top of your head between your two ears. We will return regularly to this point which is called *bai hui* (百會), or 100 returns/convergences. Have a little space between your arms and your body, and settle your weight through the centre of your feet. Keep your knees bent very slightly.

2. Spend a couple of minutes settling your body into a comfortable upright position and close your eyes.

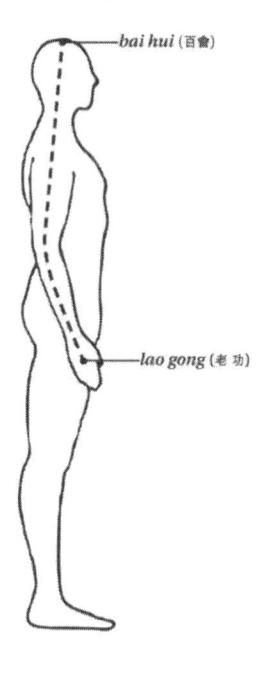

bai hui (百會)

lao gong (老功)

3. Imagine a pair of lines starting at the *bai hui* point in the crown of your head, running down the sides of your head, over your shoulders, down your arms, and along to the end of your middle fingers.

4. As you breathe in, imagine that the air enters through the *bai hui*. As you exhale, feel or imagine the breath relax the area around the *bai hui* and allow your mind to slide a few inches down the two lines.

5. Breathe into these new points down from the *bai hui*. Relax the area as you exhale and let your mind slide to a pair of points further down the lines.

6. Continue doing this until you reach the end of the middle finger. Then concentrate the mind and breathe on the centre of the palm for a minute or so. If during your descent you find that there is an area that is particularly tense, you can spend longer breathing into that area—either keep the attention there or move it down through smaller distances with each exhale.

7. Repeat this two more times.

bai hui (百會)

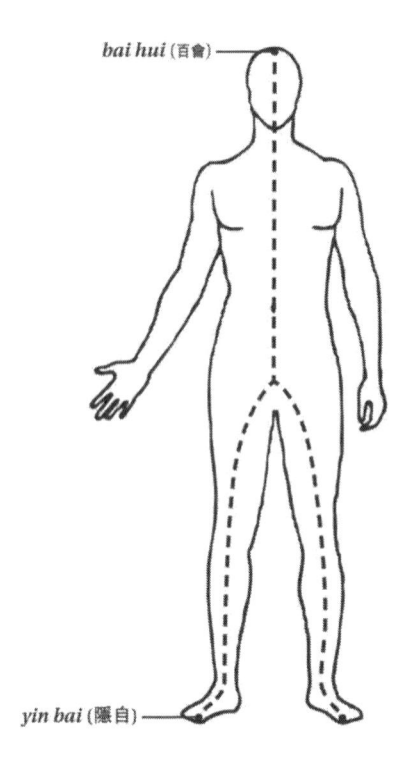

yin bai (隱白)

8. Imagine a line running from the *bai hui* down the centre of your face, chest, and belly. The line branches somewhere below the navel. The lines then run down the front of the legs to the big toes.

9. Repeat steps 4 to 7 three times using this front line to guide the mind. Keep your mind and breath at your big toes for a minute or so at the end of each line.

10. Imagine a line starting at the *bai hui* and running down the back of your body. The line branches at the sacrum, then continues down the back of the legs to the heel and the *yong chuan* (涌泉) point just behind the ball of the foot.

bai hui (百會)

yong chuan (涌泉)

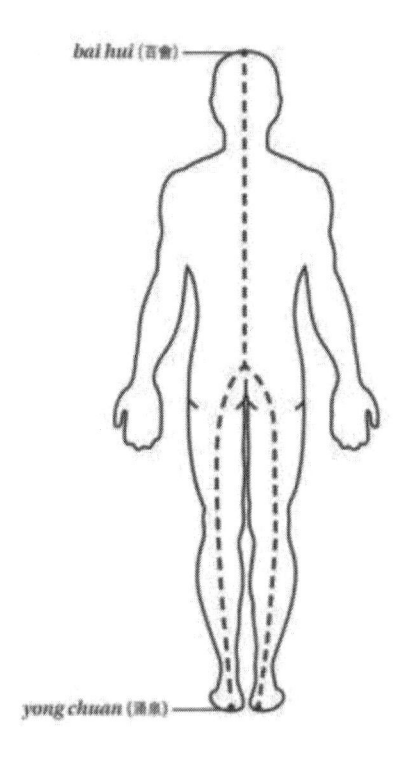

11. Repeat steps 4 to 7 three times with this line. Keep the attention and breathe at the *yong chuan* (涌泉) point for a minute or so at the end of each line.

12. Bring the attention to the lower abdomen for two to three minutes.

13. Begin to move slowly, to come back gradually to full motion. Start with your fingers, then work your way up your arms to your shoulders, then head, hips, and knees, until you are gently moving your whole body.

14. Massage any parts of your body that feel like they want the attention.

The full version of this exercise takes around 40 minutes. However, you can abbreviate this by descending the lines once or twice only. The full version will help you deepen your relaxation, while shorter versions can be used to access the deeper state.

It is important to remain upright throughout the exercises, as it will help you stay awake as you relax. Make sure that you stand in a position in which if you are startled or fall asleep and awake with a start, you are unlikely to collide with any hard or sharp objects.

Turn off any phones, alarms, or anything that is likely to make a loud noise around you. As you enter a state of profound relaxation through this exercise, it can be extremely unpleasant to be disturbed suddenly during your practise. For the same reason, it is inadvisable to practice during thunderstorms.

While this exercise helps you accumulate energy over time, it is not a substitute for sleep. If you start an exercise like this in a state of chronic stress and fatigue, it is normal for you to feel more tired than before. This results from an increase in awareness rather than an actual increase in tiredness, and is valuable information. Fortunately, increased relaxation skill improves the quality of the time you spend resting.

BASIC HAND METHODS JIBEN SHOUFA (基本手法)

Our system has 8 basic hand methods that are simple repeated movements. You find these hand movements in different combinations throughout the circular and linear forms.

Each of the basic hand methods contains various striking, defending, and locking applications.

They are not very strenuous, so work well in warm-ups. The repetition of the simple movements helps the extremities move in coordination with the centre of the body. Generally, any repetitious movement can serve to deepen body awareness and control.

1. PIERCING—CHUEN (穿)

Stand feet parallel and shoulder width apart, the right hand up level with the eyes and in line with the nose. The right palm is up, the fingers extended outward. The left hand is closed at the left hip, the palm facing downward.

From here, the right hand turns over, the fingers close, and the arm pulls down to the right hip. Simultaneously, the left hand begins to open and spiral upward until it reaches the former position of the right hand.

There is equal emphasis on the hand that draws down and the hand that pierces out. Put intention on the forearm of the rising hand, the lower edge of which should make some contact with the falling arm.

Both piercing hands finish at the same point in space at a point on a line perpendicular to the centre of the line between the two feet.

This movement includes rise, drill, overturn, and fall.

Application: Pierce and pull

Both partners standing right foot forward, right hand up.

Step forward and pierce/strike to partner's head. As partner lifts right hand to protect his head, grasp his wrist and pull down at a 45° angle on a line perpendicular to the line between the partner's heels.

We use this angle a lot in *Bagua*.

This should unbalance the partner, who can regain equilibrium by taking a step with the back (left) leg. If the partner resists the pull down, change the pull to a strike/slap to his face.

If the partner goes into "fixed step push hands mode" and resists by bending at the waist, strike the back of his exposed head with your right hand, or step in with a knee (or both).

Take care when pulling down that you do not pull your partner into you.

Application: Pierce and pull 2

This is essentially the same as above, but your partner reverses his stance, so has the left hand and foot forward.

Here you step in and pierce to his face via the inside of his left arm. This puts you in a position to pull down to your right, pulling the partner off balance backwards over his heels.

Step 1

Step 2

Step 3

Application: Counter to a grasp

Your partner grasps your right wrist with his left hand. Use your hand to pierce up to his face. The force of your pierce should be directed towards his weak angle, while the spiraling of your hand should make the partner's grip uncomfortable. This should cause the partner to either let go (and be struck in the face by your pierce) or be knocked backwards.

2. CHOPPING—KAN (砍)

Step 1
(step 1-5 front view, step 6-11 side view)

Start feet parallel shoulder width apart, hands raised to shoulder height, arms rounded, palms facing each other.

Step 2

Turn the right foot in, moving the right hip, shoulder, and hand in coordination so the right hand scoops along the inside of the left forearm. The right knee should be bent with the majority of weight on the right foot.

Step 3

Push off the right foot so the weight moves into the left leg and the body leans forward slightly. At the same time, the left hand arcs out to the left, and the right hand arcs out to the right.

To repeat on the other side, turn the left foot in to the left while scooping the left hand along the inside of the right forearm to the elbow. Then push off the left leg and open the arms as on the other side.

Step 4

Step 5

Step 6
(step 1-5 front view, step 6-11 side view)

Step 7
(step 1-3 front view, step 4-8 side view)

Step 8

Step 9

Step 10

Step 11

Application: Chopping

Both partners standing right foot forward, right hand up.

Step forward and chop down at 45° to the right side of your partner's head with your right hand. Your partner should raise his right hand to defend himself.

Bring your left hand under your right to grab your partner's right wrist.

Step in once more while using your left hand to pull your partner out to your left along his weak angle. This frees your right hand to eagerly continue chopping towards the right side of your partner's head/neck.

If your partner lifts his left hand to defend, repeat the last movement, stepping in and clearing his left hand with yours, and chopping with the right. Hopefully by then he will run out of hands!

Step 1

Step 2

Alternative: After the initial contact right hand to right hand, use your left hand to slap your partner's right elbow down to his weak angle at 45°, which clears the way to step in and strike again.

Step 1

Step 2

You can also practice this from the outside if your partner starts with a left lead.

Step 1

Step 2

Step 3

Application: From a grasp

Your partner grabs your right wrist with his left hand.

Maintaining a rounded posture with your right arm, roll around the point of contact while pulling his palm into your wrist with your left hand. You can keep this pressure on to damage his wrist, or clear his hand with your left hand and chop to his head with your right.

3. PUSHING—TUI (推)

Starting feet shoulder width apart and feet parallel, the right hand is palm up at the right hip, the left hand is extended out in front of the centre of the chest, the wrist settled so the fingers are higher than the palm which faces outwards.

From here, turn the left palm over to face upwards and swing the right arm around in an arc so that the hand is higher than the head. The forearm should be vertical, as if hanging from the wrist. The right palm is parallel to the ground with the fingers pointing forward.

Next, the right elbow drops forward, followed by the forearm. Finally, the right wrist settles so that the palm faces forward and the fingers upward.

As this happens, the left hand withdraws to the hip.

As the right hand descends, it brushes the withdrawing left hand. Keep intention in the right forearm as it descends, moving it to the palm in the end.

Pushing- Tui ((推) front view

The obvious application of this movement is a forward palm strike, the wrist adding a final crispness while changing the angle of impact, making it harder to deal with.

Alternatively, use your right hand to grasp inside the partner's right elbow. Pull your right hand back and down to break their structure, circling it up to bear down on your partner with your forearm.

Step 1

Step 2

Step 3

Step 4

Step 5

Application: Practice whole body stepping

Description:

To get a sense of how to use the weight of the body when striking rather than the arm, try this practice. Stand in *ho tien shi* (後天式) about one meter from a partner, who stands sideways on. Your partner should tense their neck slightly to prevent it from being jolted on impact.

Keep your forward arm very straight, take a step towards your partner with your front foot, drawing up the rear foot behind you immediately. Your palm should collide with your partner's shoulder.

Keep your striking arm straight so that you are not tempted to use it to either hit or push your partner. Bring the rear leg and weight up immediately on impact. Let your entire body feel like a hammer striking a gong.

If you maintain good body alignment, you will finish in the same position as you started, and your partner will be knocked away by your momentum. If you lose your alignment, you will notice what parts of your body are most affected by the force of the collision and be able to correct them another time.

The receiving partner should stand naturally and not try to either resist or go with the impact. This way, they will also be able to give better feedback on the quality of the impact.

Obviously, when you really strike someone, it is not necessary or desirable to maintain such a stiff and formal position. However, you can use this practice to develop your ability to align and ground force on impact.

Ho tien shi (後天式)

Step 1

Step 2

Step 3

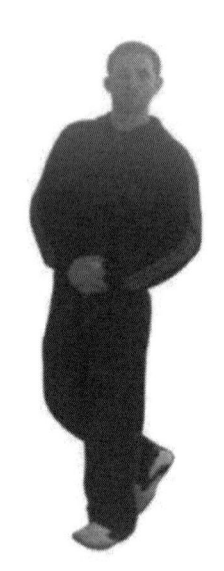

Step 4

4. CRASHING—ZHUANG (撞)

Starting feet parallel and shoulder width apart, the right hand opens at the right hip, palm facing forwards and fingers pointing downwards.

The left palm extends outwards in line with the centre, level with the solar plexus, and the fingers point upwards.

The left elbow is dropped and the forearm is parallel to the floor. From here, the right elbow urges the right palm forward, which turns as it advances.

It rubs over the left forearm as it goes, ending in the position of the left forearm above.

At the same time, the left forearm withdraws, turning over as it goes until it is in the original position of the right forearm.

The forward movement of the palm is often used as a straight palm strike.

Application: From a grasp

If grasped on the right wrist by your partner's right hand, the withdrawing motion can be used to break his grip and unbalance him across his weak angle, followed by a strike to the groin.

A similar technique can be used if grasped on the right wrist by the opponent's left hand. Either withdraw and strike back with the right hand or simultaneously withdraw the right and strike with the left.

Step 1

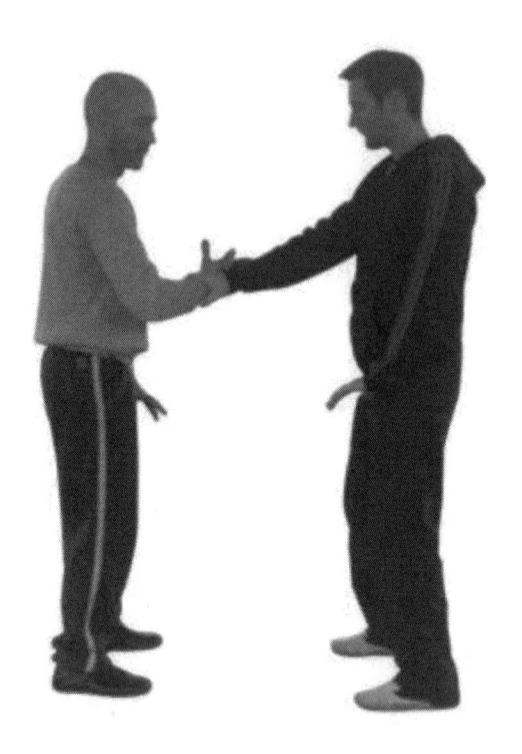

Step 2

Step 3

Step 4

Step 5

Xian tien Bagua (先天 八卦掌)

Xian tien Bagua contains all the circle walking and the circular palm changes the art is known for.

    Metaphorically, our *xian tien Bagua* is like a dragon. The head is the single palm change, the body is the eight palm changes, and the tail is a set of changes called *wulong bai wei* (烏龍擺尾)—the black dragon swings its tail.

Single palm change contains the essence of *Bagua*, so it is the head of the dragon. The essence is elaborated in the eight palm changes that make the body. These elaborations are then condensed into a smoother version in the tail.

While there are many martial applications in the *xian tien* palm changes, the main emphasis is on a smooth, balanced quality of movement and a twisting, stretching of the body to develop power.

In fact, every step, hand circle, or body movement can be seen as some kind of kick, strike, evasion, or throw. However, trying to practice them overtly as such defeats the purpose of the exercise.

Basic Circle Walking

Circle walking, whether done with fixed hand postures or active changes, is the core of most *Bagua* systems.

The idea is that circle walking develops balance, mobility, internal connection, and can also be used as meditation.

When starting circle walking, it is best to take time and be clear about certain points.

The head needs to lift and the waist to settle. The hands can be folded together below the navel. This keeps the centre of gravity low, and allows the attention to go to the feet and weight.
Especially when starting out, it is useful to pause at the moment where the feet pass each other. One foot carries all the weight, the other is held parallel to the floor and just above it. The feeling is that the whole body gathers and drops into the supporting leg. We call this step the chicken step, or *ji bu* (雞步). It not only develops balance, but helps put weight into strikes.

From here, the unweighted foot slides forward, skimming the floor with some sensitivity as if rolling pencils with the sole. At the point where it can extend no further without shifting the weight into it, the foot can be put down.

The outside foot hooks in slightly at the end of each step. The inside foot steps forward parallel with the line of the outside foot.

The amount the outside foot hooks in depends on the size of the circle. The smaller the circle you walk, the more tightly you will need to hook. A typical circle is 8 to 12 steps around. In really tight circles (2 to 4 steps), it is also normal to turn the inside foot out.

How far you step is determined by how deeply you can sit in the leg that supports the weight. This in turn depends on thigh strength and knee and ankle flexibility. Walking is often classified into three levels: high, which is similar to normal walking; middle, where there is some bend in the knees; and low, where the thighs are parallel to the ground. The last one requires considerable leg strength and flexibility.

Approaches to practice

When starting a training session, you can begin in two ways. In the first, you try to be perfect from the first movement. This is tricky, and puts considerable psychological stress on the beginning of each session.

The alternative is to start casually, knowing that it takes time to tune in and get it right. Psychologically, this is much easier.

Sometimes I avoid training because I put heavy demands on myself. I imagine myself doing some graceful, extended, or strenuous movement, and somewhere inside, there is resistance. My body says, "No, I don't want to do that now!" When I do start to practice, the difference between what I imagine myself doing and how it actually feels can be so great that I often give up in disgust after a short time.

If I just start to play around, soon enough I begin to develop curiosity about and enthusiasm for more precise, demanding movements. When I start practice this way, I usually run out of time and still want to do more.

Generally, human beings learn most easily through play. By starting with an attitude of fun and pleasure, you support your personal practice.

As a session develops, it is ordinary for your concentration to deepen and for you to be more absorbed in the practice.

Because training, especially slow training, can lead to sensations of deep comfort and peace, often when mentally agitated, it is tempting to do slow practice. Often what happens is that the physical stillness just throws the mental agitation into a starker relief.

In this case, it is often more helpful to pace the mental activity with more vigorous physical training, and then slow down. When paced physically, the mental activity will often calm as the body tempo slow down.

Just as you can start slowly, or quickly, you can also start (too) tense, or too relaxed. If you start too tense, gradually adjust your body to an optimal relaxation. If you start too floppy, gradually add in more tone.

Make minimal adjustments during this process. Don't shake out the whole body because the hand is a bit tight. Rather, use your mind to become aware of the connected areas and relax them as you can.

600 Steps

This is a training method for circle walking based on the idea of starting easily and casually, then becoming more precise.

The 600 steps are divided into three sections. The first 200 (about 10 circles each way) are done in a very relaxed way. Like taking a stroll in the park, kicking stones, and enjoying the scenery.

For the next 200, begin to bend the knees more and pay more attention to the soles of the feet—start to walk in a more formal *Bagua* manner.

For the final 200, raise the hands to one of the fixed postures.

This need not take long. You can complete 600 steps in as quickly as 10 minutes. Sometimes you may want to slow down, each step taking half a minute. If, after you have completed your 600, you want to keep going, then you are free to continue…

Single Palm Change

Dan huan zhang (單換掌), or single palm change, is a key pattern within *Gao* style and many other systems of *Bagua*. What I mean by this is that you can see all the other movement of the system as combinations of components of single palm change. At first, this may seem an intellectual concept, but with practise, it becomes ingrained into the body.

When you physically appreciate that all the movements and applications have a single root, it makes it easier to learn, remember, and change between movements. If everything is single palm change, then the change is between something and itself—you find the constant in the variable.

How does single palm change include all of the movements of the system?

Single palm change contains *kou* (鈎) steps and *bai* (擺) steps. There are closing and opening movements, the hands separate and cross, go up and down, and move to the inside and to the outside. Circle palm change contains arcs in three planes of circle, horizontal, vertical, and diagonal.

You can take any of these movements and make them bigger or smaller, lower or higher, add or take away steps, and repeat them to the inside or outside. It goes back to the theory of the *yijing* (易經) as applied to Bagua.

As such, single palm change is very important throughout the training syllabus; especially at the beginning where it supplies the basics, and at the end where it encompasses all of the other movements.

This is the reason I do not give any specific applications for singe palm change. All applications are single palm change. It also explains why in the system we do not emphasize any particular part of the movement. The power needs to be smooth, balanced, and constant throughout. This way, it trains the potential for expression in any direction at any time, as well as the capacity for change.

The most basic way to practice single palm change is to hold each of the positions. This allows time to pay attention to details, tire the legs, and still the mind. It can also be practised smoothly, slowly, or quickly.

Xian tien shi (先天式)—Pre-Heaven Stance

1. Stand feet together, arms by the sides.

2. Raise the arms over the head and sit down onto the right leg.

3. Turn the hips to the left and slide the left foot forward while the hands slide downwards, as if slipping along an imaginary pole.

4. Finish with the fingers of the left hand at eye level, the first two fingers vertical, the thumb open, and the palm slightly hollow. The eyes gaze into the space between the thumb and fingers. The right hand is vertical with the fingers pointing at the left elbow about a hand's length below it. The weight is 90% to 100% on the right leg, the knee bent, and the spine vertical.

5. Twist both hands forwards so that there is a sense of the thumbs lifting up the centre line. Balance the forward force of the hands with a backwards force in the spine.

6. Once you have established this position, relax as much as you can.

Single Palm Change—Dan Huan Zhang (單換掌)

1. Shift the weight forward into the left leg, pick up the right foot, and take a *kou* step in front of the left leg. The upper body remains unchanged.

2. Shift the weight into the right foot and lift the left heel, then turn the waist to the left, continuing until you have turned through 180°. The left hand turns so that the fingers are horizontal and the palm faces out.

3. Shift the weight forward and step past the left foot with the right foot. Keep the right foot pointing straight ahead and the weight in the left leg. Turn the hips to the left and turn the left foot out while maintaining the knee in the same direction as the foot. The left hand remains largely in place while the right palm pushes horizontally under the left armpit.

4. Rotate back to the right with the weight still in the left foot. The right fingers drill upwards at a 45° angle and the right hand slides along the underside of the left forearm, continuing the line of movement upwards and outwards before falling back to the original position in 1.

Pre-Heaven Palm Changes 1–4

Even within the *Gao* style, there are a number of different variations as to how to do the forms. The variations that I describe here are what Luo laoshi teaches to students. In some styles of *Bagua*, palm changes follow the line of the circle. In the *Gao* style, some changes follow the line of the circle, others are tangential to it, some changes cross it, others enter to the centre and exit again, and still others exit the circle and return.

Each of the palm changes relates to one line of the *ho tien* forms. I have included some applications with each form, though I repeat a good part of the *xian tien* training is focused on quality of movement through different directions rather than developing some specific use.

Many of these applications are throws, and for a more in-depth view of throwing which was influenced by our system, I refer you to Tim Cartmell's excellent book Effortless Combat Throws.

(steps 1-10 front view, steps 11-20 side view)

(steps 1-10 front view, steps 11-20 side view)

(steps 1-10 front view, steps 11-20 side view)

(steps 1-10 front view, steps 11-20 side view)

Snake Form Smooth Body Palm *she xing xun huan zhang* (蛇形順勢掌)

115

In this palm change, the body turns, then shifts between the left and right foot while descending into a deep, extended stance. The shifting while descending has a snake-like rhythm to it.

The health benefit of this form is to act on heart fire.

1. Start in *xian tien shi*, left step forward, and take a *bai* step to the outside with the right foot. At the same time, rotate the left forearm inwards, dropping the elbow slightly.

Step 1a

Step 1b

Step 1c

Step 1d

2. Keep the upper body position fixed and take a *kou* step with the left foot so that the body has rotated through 360° from the first position.

Step 2a

Step 2b

Step 2c

Step 3

3. Shift the weight to the right foot and begin to coil the right hand under the armpit following the little finger side and with the palm facing upwards.

Step 3a

4. Shift the weight back to the left, and continue coiling with the right hand.

Step 4

5. Sit down into the left leg, extending the right foot out with the right arm in line with the right leg. Keep the left knee pushed out over the left foot during this movement, and aim to approach vertical with the spine.

Step 5a

Step 5b

6. Scoop the left hand over the head towards the right knee by turning the body to the right. Continue the scooping movement, finishing by pushing the left palm out with the fingers pointing down. The left arm and right arms should be in line with the spine straight and a leaning to approach horizontal. During this movement, some weight follows the hand towards the right, and then back to the left again.

Step 6a

Step 6b

Step 6c

Step 6d

7. Pierce to the right with the right hand while the left leg twists inwards and straightens out. The weight moves into the right leg. The left palm pushes through until the fingers point up to the right elbow.

Step 7a

Step 7b

Step 7c

Step 7d

8. Continue piercing upwards with the right hand while turning the body to the left. Pull the left leg up and past the right foot, placing it straight forwards. The left hand strokes under the right forearm, continuing past until the body rests in the original position 1.

Step 8a

Step 8b

Step 8c

To change sides, do a single palm change with a delayed step.

Step 1

Step 2

Step 3

Step 4

Step 5

Step 6

Step 7

Application: Throw

The following is a sample of how to use the smooth body snake form palm change to execute a throw. A technique like this can have many variations to be used in different situations.

A grabs B around the neck with his left hand.

B pulls A's elbow close to his chest so that A's balance is disrupted.

B steps forward and to the right of A's left shoulder.

B leans forward, turns his body to the right, and uses his left shoulder to knock A even further off balance. B places his left hand across A's left hip to prevent him from moving his feet so that he falls.

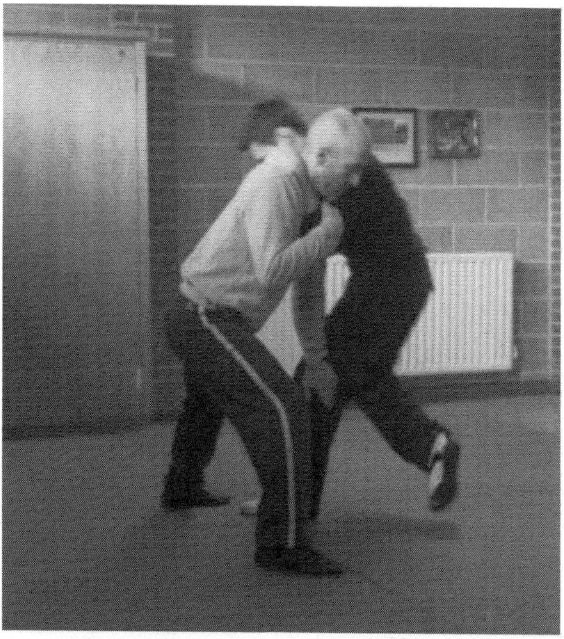

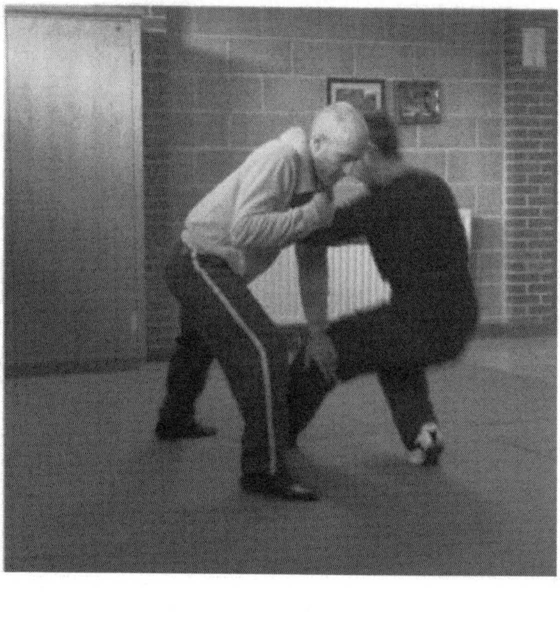

Dragon Shape Piercing Hand Palm *long xing chuan shou zhang* (龍形穿手掌)

Snakes and dragons are similar. A dragon is basically a giant snake that can fly, so there are some strong similarities between the two forms. The dragon form starts with a horizontal movement that turns into a separation towards above and below. After some transition, the form becomes like the snake form.

The health benefit of this form is to regulate the triple burner.

1. Start in *xian tien shi* with the left foot forward and the left hand facing into the centre of the circle.

Step 1

2. Shift the weight forward and take a *kou* step into the centre of the circle with the right foot.

Step 2

3. Step in towards the centre of the circle with the left foot and turn the left hand palm up to pierce at the same time. The right hand continues to support the left a hand's with below the left elbow.

Step 3a

Step 3b

4. Shift forwards to take a *kou* step with the right foot in front of the left foot, and with the right palm down, move the hand around to the left side of the body.

Step 4a

Step 4B

Step 4c

5. Lift the left hand upwards and slide the right palm along the left side of the waist, chest, and then up the left arm until it is higher than the left hand.

Step 5a

Step 5b

6. Turn the body to the right and start sliding the left palm down the now extended right arm.

Step 6

7. Once you have turned the body to the right, and the left hand has reached the right shoulder/armpit, begin to drop the body onto the right leg. The left knee points to the ground and the left heel raises up. The left hand points to the floor with the palm facing out and in the bend of the right hip.

Step 7

8. Keeping the right hand extended up to the ceiling, turn the body 180° to the left. The right knee finishes pointing to the floor with the right heel raised and the left foot flat on the floor. The left palm faces out, slightly to the outside of the left knee, with the fingers pointing downwards.

Step 8a

Step 8b

Step 8c

9. Shift the weight back into the right foot and step directly behind with the left foot while coiling the left hand under, extending it along the line of the left leg, palm up. The right hand drops slightly. The weight stays in the right leg. You are now in position 5 of snake above, but on the opposite side.

Step 9a

Step 9b

Step 9c

10. Scoop the right hand over towards the left knee by turning the body to the left. Continue the scooping movement, finishing by pushing the right palm out with the fingers pointing down. The left arm and right arms should be in line, with the spine straight and a leaning to approach horizontal. During this movement, some weight follows the hand towards the left, and then back to the right again.

Step 10a

Step 10b

Step 10c

11. Pierce to the left with the left hand while the right leg twists inwards and straightens out. The weight moves into the left leg. The right palm pushes through until the fingers point up to the left elbow.

Step 11

12. Continue piercing upwards with the left hand while turning the body to the left. Pull the right leg up and past the left foot, placing it straight to the right along the line of the circle. The right hand strokes under the right forearm, continuing past until the body rests back in *xian tien shi* with the right foot forward and right hand extended into the circle.

Step 12a

Step 12b

Step 12c

Application: Throw

Dragon Form

The throw that follows is common in many martial arts. It is shown here set up with a chop as is found in the section on basic hand methods. There is also a follow-up change shown in case of resistance.

B steps in to chop towards the right side of A's neck using his right hand.

Upon being blocked, B pulls A's left hand down and out at 45° to off-balance him and create an opening to reach around the left side of A's neck.

B then steps further in, he turns his right foot in, wraps his right arm around the back of A's neck, and pulls A's tight hand close to his body using his left hand.

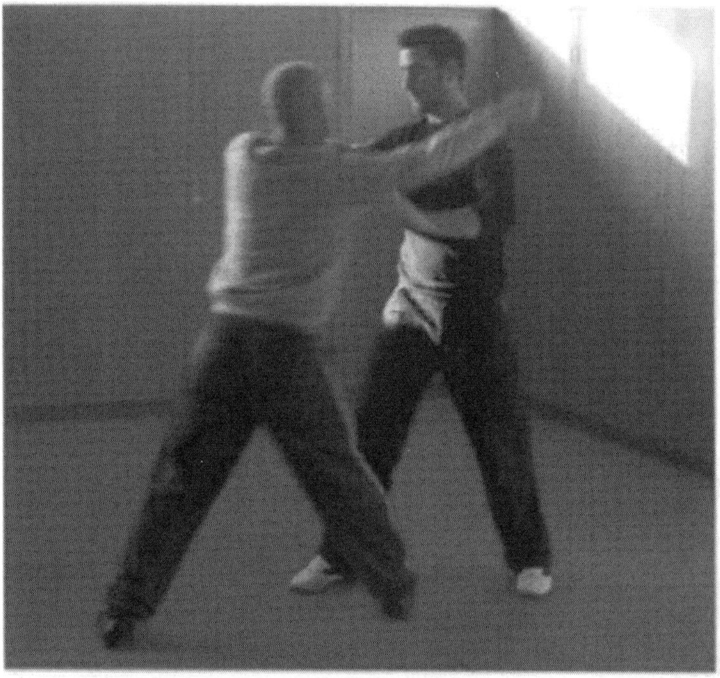

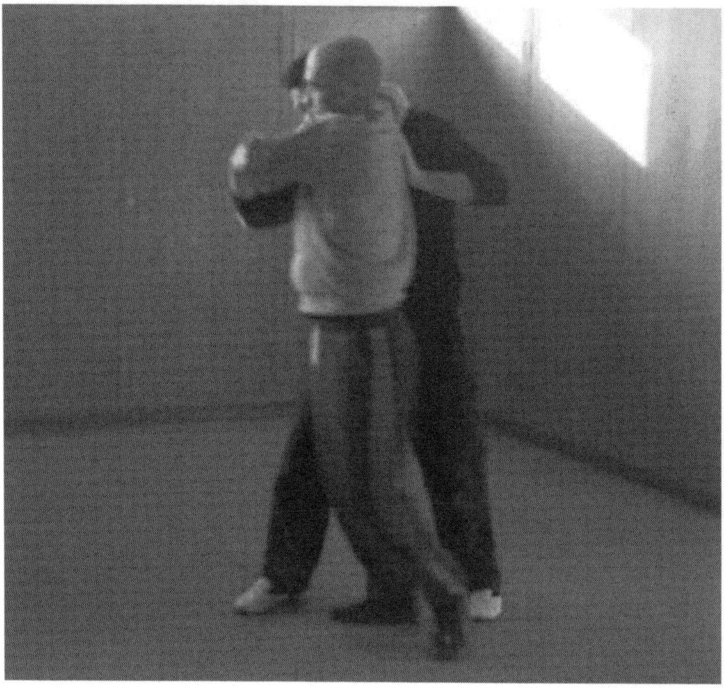

B bends his knees slightly to place his lower back next to and across A's hips.

B continues to turn and pull A's hand and neck so that A falls onto B's lower back.

As B straightens his legs, A is thrown.

If B wraps his right arm around A's neck, but finds that A is in a position to resist his throw, A can change directions.

B uses his right hand to lever A's head up and back, then towards the floor. At the same time, B steps around to his left with his left, then right foot. The resultant rotation pulls A off balance and down.

You will notice that B has his left hand raised. This can be to strike, to threaten a strike, or to convince the gullible that it is the empty force of the left hand that caused the fall.

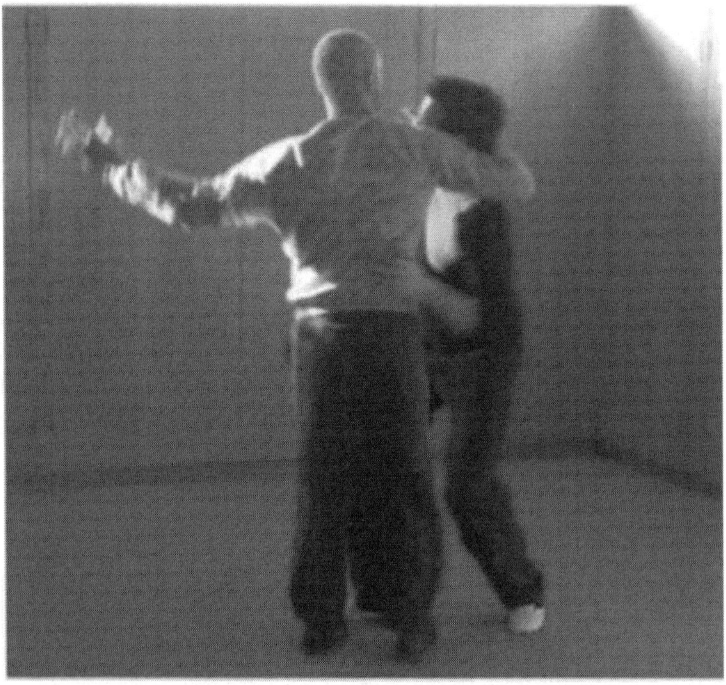

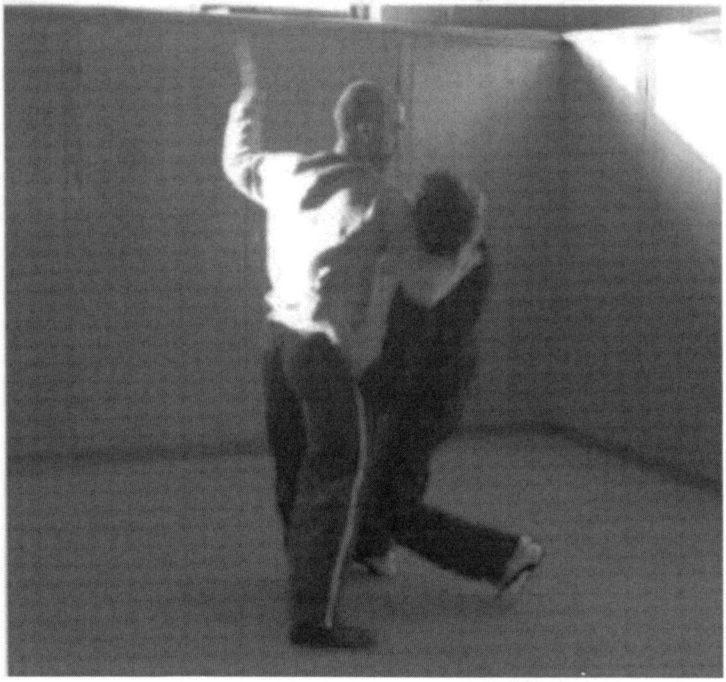

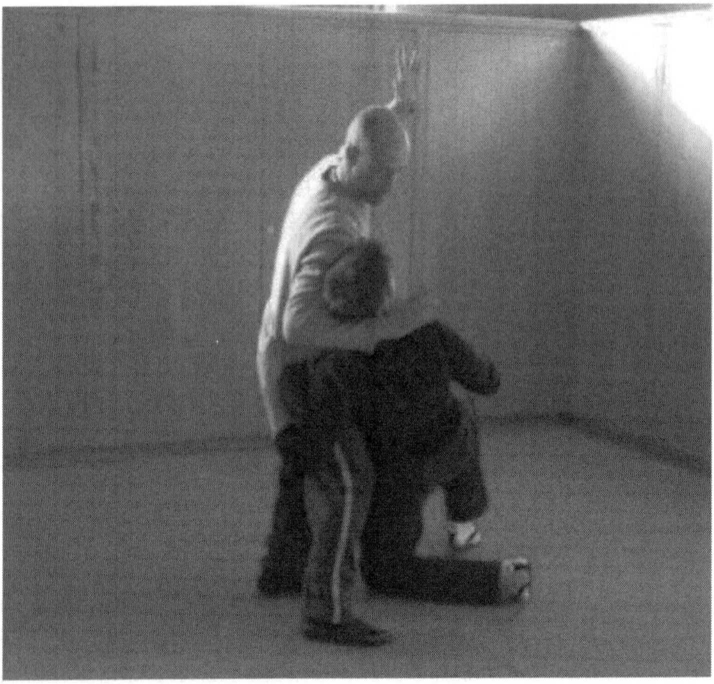

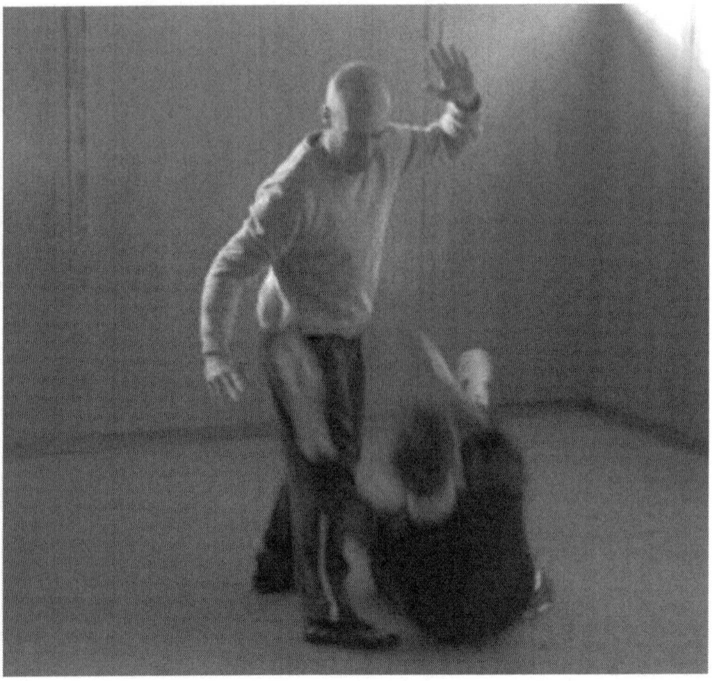

Returning Body Strike—The Tiger Palm
Hwei shen da hu zhang (回身打虎掌)

This palm change uses a number of movements where the weight drops into the palm. It is this dropping of the weight which is supposed to resemble a pouncing tiger.

This form is said to benefit the stomach and lungs.

1. Start in *xian tien shi* with the left foot forward and the left hand facing into the centre of the circle.

2. Shift the weight forward to take a *bai* step to the outside with the right foot, drop the left elbow slightly, and turn the forearm in so that the left forearm and fingers point directly upwards. The right hand continues to support the left elbow.

Step 1

Step 2

Step 3

3. Take a *kou* step around with the left foot and begin to slide the right palm up the left forearm. Turn the body to the right and sit into the left foot while raising the right heel. With the *kou* and *bai* step, you should have turned through 360°.

Step 3a

Step 3b

4. Keep sliding the right hand past the end of the left forearm and begin to lean back slightly.

Step 4

5. Rotate the right palm around the right centre of the right forearm in the vertical plane so it comes down on the inside of the left hand with the palm facing out and down. The right elbow is slightly higher than the left palm, which has turned to face outwards.

Step 5

6. Take a half step forwards with the right foot. The body leans to the right slightly while the weight finishes 70% in the left foot. The right hand is in line with the right foot, turned so the fingers point downwards, the palm faces out, and the thumb points to the right. The left hand supports the right elbow, palm outwards, fingers pointing upwards.

Step 6a

Step 6b

7. Shift the weight 90% into the right foot and raise the body up a little, then sit down and turn to the left. The body leans slightly to the left, and the left hand extends out along the line of the left foot, the palm facing out, the fingers down and the thumb pointing to the left.

Step 7a

Step 7b

Step 7c

8. Pierce to the left with the left hand while the right leg twists inwards and straightens out. The weight moves into the left leg. The right palm pushes through until the fingers point up to the left elbow.

Step 8a

Step 8b

9. Continue piercing upwards with the left hand while turning the body to the left. Pull the right leg up and past the left foot, placing it straight to the right along the line of the circle. The right hand strokes under the right forearm, continuing past until the body rests back in *xian tien shi* with the right foot forward and right hand extended into the circle.

Step 9a

Step 9b

Step 9c

Step 9d

Application: Throw

Tiger Form

The following application comes from the initial rotation at the beginning of this palm change.

A places his right hand to grasp the back of B's neck. B tilts his head slightly to the left to trap A's hand in place as he twist rapidly to the right.

B's left arm rises on a diagonal as if to clout the right side of A's head and lock out A's elbow.

B then takes a slight *kou* step around the centre point between the two bodies with his right foot and turns sharply to his left while he uses his left hand to hook A's elbow and applies a force at 45° down towards the ground.

As A attempts to regain his balance, B lifts his left foot to prevent A from stepping, which makes A fall. Throughout this movement, B has his right hand ready to strike A.

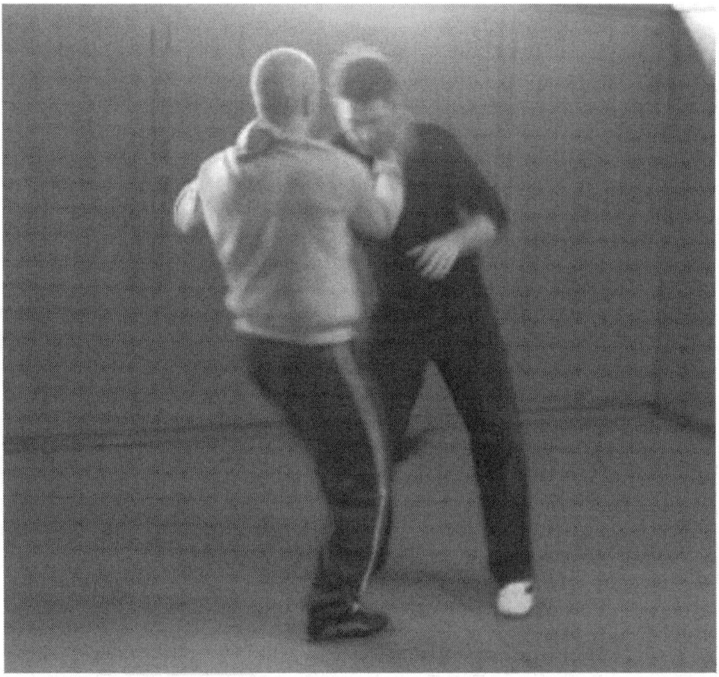

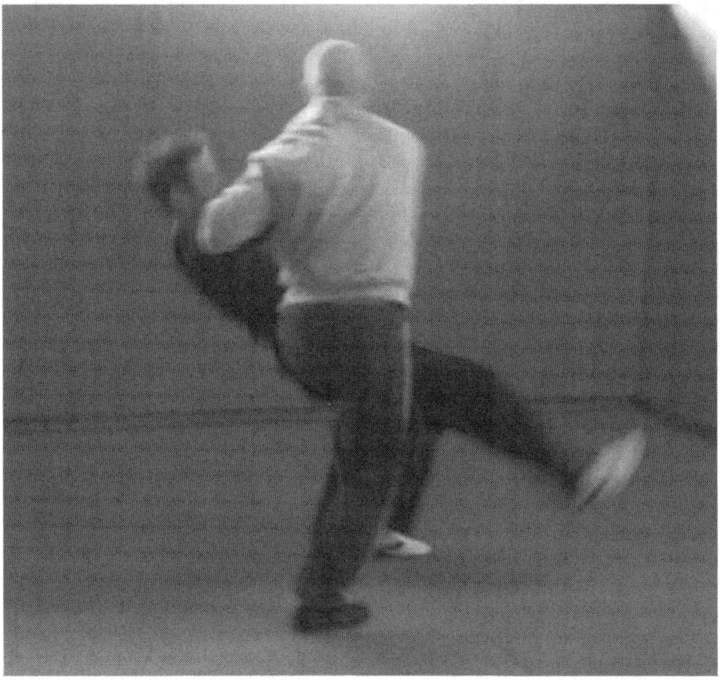

Swallow Form Overturning Body Palm
Yan xing gai shou zhang (燕翻蓋手掌)

This form is said to benefit the kidneys.

1 Start in *xian tien shi* with the left foot forward and the left hand facing into the centre of the circle.

2. Shift the weight forward and take a slight *kou* step with the right foot in front of the left.

3. Shift the weight into the right foot and lift the left palm so that it faces up just above eye level with the fingers pointing into the centre of the circle. The right hand also lifts so that the palms face up and the fingers point along the same line as those of the left hand. The right thumb points out.

Step 1

Step 2

4. Step towards the centre of the circle with the left foot. At the same time, coil the left hand in towards the centre of the circle so that the palm faces up while scooping with the right hand so that the palm faces up at the level of the hip and the fingers are in the same line as those of the left hand.

Step 4

Step 5

5. Shift the weight forward into the left foot, take a *bai* step forwards with the right foot, then step behind again with the left foot. At the same time, pierce the right hand downwards over the left forearm.

6. Keep extending the left hand in the same direction across the circle, and using the sensation of being pulled by the right hand, rotate the body around the spine, which leans diagonally. The weight remains in the right foot. The left foot helps maintain balance until the last moment where the knee pulls up under the left elbow. The left palm faces up and the fingers point straight forward.

In the overturning movement, there is the sensation of opening through the left side as the body turns, then the left side closing as the left foot lifts off the ground.

Step 6a

Step 6b

Step 6c

Step 6d

Step 6e

Step 6f

Step 6g

Step 6h

Step 6i

Step 6h

7. Pierce forwards with the left hand and place the left foot down on the ground on the opposite side of the circle to which you started. The weight moves into the left leg. The right palm pushes through until the fingers point up to the left elbow.

Step 7a

Step 7b

8. Continue piercing upwards with the left hand while turning the body to the left. Pull the right leg up and past the left foot, placing it to the right along the line of the circle. The right hand strokes under the right forearm, continuing past until the body rests back in *xian tien shi* with the right foot forward and right hand extended into the circle.

Step 8a

Step 8b

Application: Throw

Swallow Form

The following application starts with the now familiar chop opening.

B chops towards A with his right hand. A uses the position with his hands on the inside of A's to twist A's right elbow inwards, which misaligns his body.

At the same time, B's right hand opens slightly down and to the right to create enough space to reach A's head.

B then pushes A's head back with his right hand.

A will have trouble resisting if the initial misalignment of his right elbow has taken place.

B maintains the twist on A's elbow and the pressure on A's head as he steps up to place his left foot behind A's right knee.

This collapses the knee, which now completely destroys A's stability and causes him to fall.

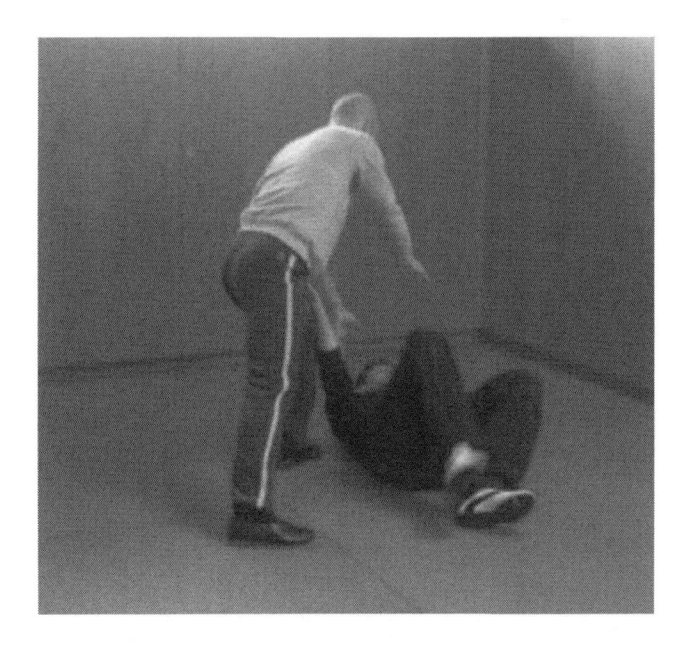

Final words

Thank you for reading this first book. I trust that you have found useful information in it. I learned a great deal in writing it that I plan to apply in the next books (which are well underway).

I recognize that this book is a long way from perfect. The ability to go on despite a the lack of perfection is vital to progress in any skill. Do your practice today, notice what is good and notice what is less good. Accept both and find ways to improve.

This idea is embedded in the structure of Bagua, and not just in the idea of daily practice. It is present in the martial tactics. It is found in the ability to change when a technique does not work as expected, to accept and move on. It is found in the way the movements are put together, poised and balanced to shift direction.

In Bagua you expect things to go 'wrong' so you train to use the unexpected. Bagua, like life is constant movement, constant change.

I have been practicing for more than twenty years now. Everyday and every step is a learning opportunity. As long as I practice I cannot stop learning, though I cannot control what I learn. In fact the less I try to control what I learn the more that I do learn.

If you want to get the most from this book, practice. Step off the page and into movement. Move and keep moving. Get it wrong again and again and learn each time. Experiment, learn and become your own authority.

Chinese Glossary

Ba duan jin (八段錦): 8 pieces of brocade; a series of 8 breathing exercises of which are commonly practiced in many traditions and which exist with many variations.

Ba mu zhang (八母掌): 8 mother palms; 8 fixed hand positions held during circle walking to develop structure and as meditation.

Bagua (八卦): 8 trigrams; a trigram consists of a combination of three broken or unbroken lines, one above the other. Broken lines denote yin, unbroken lines denote yang. The 8 trigrams are an important part of the binary system that is at the base of the yijing.

Baguazhang (八卦掌): 8 trigram palm.

Bai hui (百會): 100 convergences; an acupuncture point at the top of the head, between the ears.

Bai (擺): To swing; bai bu (擺步) refers to steps where the foot is turned outwards.

Ban bu (半步): Half step; a step in which the front foot moves forward while the back foot trails behind.

Chen (陳): the family name of the oldest known style of Taijiquan.

Chen shi Taijiquan (陳式太極拳): the chen style of Taijiquan.

Chuen (穿): to pierce, a movement found in various Gao style Bagua forms, exercises and techniques.

Dan huan zhang (單換掌): Single palm change; the key movement of Bagua that can be stretched, shortened, repeated, or reversed to form any of the other movements.

Dan-tien (丹田): The field of the elixir; an area in the lower abdomen of the body, which roughly corresponds to the centre of gravity, and is also used as a focus of concentration in breathing and meditation exercises.

Dun (囤): To lower; the name of the third straight line palm change of GSB.

Fang song (放鬆): To relax.

Fang song gong (放鬆功): Relaxing exercise or skill.

Gao Yi Sheng (高義盛): The founder of this style of Bagua.

Hotien shi (後天式): Post-heaven posture; the basic starting posture of linear GSB that can be held to develop body structure and for meditation.

Ho tien (後天): Post heaven; refers to the dynamic state of change that occurs in the real world (compared to the ideal state of xian tien) embodied in the 64 straight line palm changes of Gao style Bagua.

Ji bu (雞步): Chicken step; a stepping method in which the balance is held clearly on one foot, while the other foot is held above and parallel to the ground just next to the supporting foot.

Jiben shoufa (基本手法): Basic hand methods; a series of 8 exercises to develop body structure, rhythm, smoothness of movement, and martial application in GSB.

Jigoro Kano (嘉納治五郎): The founder of Judo. Judo (柔道): Soft way Japanese martial sport.

Judoka (柔道家): a practitioner of Judo.

Kai (開): To open; the name of the first straight line palm change of GSB.

Kan (砍): to chop, a movement found in various Gao style Bagua forms, exercises and techniques.

Kou (鈎): To hook; kou bu (鈎步) is a hook step, a step where the foot is turned inwards.

Lao ba zhang (老八掌): 8 old palms; the 8 palm changes practiced in circular xian tien Bagua.

Laoshi (老師): The Chinese term for teacher.

Luo Dexiu (羅德修): 5th generation practitioner of Bagua; my teacher.

Luo laoshi (羅老師): Teacher Luo.

Neigong (內功): Internal training; exercises that train the deep structure of the body in coordination with the mind; an intention.

peng (掤): In Taiji, a quality of unified body use that channels force down into the ground while relaxation is maintained.

Peng (捧): To uphold; the name of the second straight line palm change of GSB.

Qi eo (氣油): Petrol; literally breath oil.

Qi (氣): Breath or energy.

Qigong (氣功): Breathing exercises.

Sheng qi (生氣): Angry; literally birth breath.

Taiji (太極): Extreme pole; a Chinese concept of complementary exchange between yin and yang, and also the name of Chinese martial art (taijiquan).

Taijiquan (陳式太極拳): A Chinese martial art originating in the Chen family village in Henan province documented back to the 17th Century.

Tan (探): To test; the name of the fourth straight line palm change of GSB.

Tien gan (天干): Heavenly stems; an idea from Chinese astrology that is used as a name for a series of 10 body conditioning exercises in GSB.

Tien qi (天氣): Weather; literally heaven/sky breath.

Tui (推): to push a movement found in various Gao style Bagua forms, exercises and techniques.

Wulong bai hui (烏龍擺尾): Black dragon waves its tail; a palm change that encapsulates other circular palm changes of Gao style Bagua.

Xian tien shi (先天式): pre-heaven posture; the most common fixed posture in circular GSB, which can be held to develop structure and as meditation.

Xian tien (先天): Pre-heaven; refers to an ideal state of balance which is embodied in the circle walking and circular palm changes of Gao style Bagua.

Yang Luchan (楊露禪): The founder of Yang style Taiji renowned for his fighting skill.

Yijing (易經): The Chinese classic of change from which the trigrams come from, and which forms a philosophical base for Bagua.

Yoga nidra: An Indian term – literally yogic sleep.

Yong chuan (涌泉): Bubbling well; an acupuncture point on the sole of the foot.

Zhan zhuang (站桩): Post standing; the exercise of holding a fixed posture while standing to develop structure and as meditation.

Zhuang (撞): to crash; a movement found in various Gao style Bagua forms, exercises and techniques.

About the author

Edward Hines was born in London in 1968. He started boxing with St Pancras boys club when he was nine years old and Zheng Manqing Taiji aged 15 in 1983.

In 1991 Edward moved to Taiwan to pursue his Taiji studies. His primary Teacher during his time there was Dr Tao Pingxiang, he also studied with Liu Hseheng.

It was during this time that Edward met renowned Bagua master Luo Dexiu. He became an indoor student of Luo in 1993 and maintains close relations with him. Edward also learned Hebei Xingyiquan and Chen Panling Taiji with Luo.

Edward returned to England in 1994

During his time in England Edward entered tournaments, to win national titles in form, push hands and full contact fighting (San Da) while investigating other forms of martial arts and fitness.

While Edward has specialized knowledge in the Chinese styles of Baguazhang, Taijiquan, and Xingyiquan he has also spent time training in or exchanging with practitioners of Aikido, Aunkai, Simbha Sansho, Pencak Silat, Pancrase, Savate, Wing Chun (in many of its various spellings) la Cane, Jeet Kune Do, Medieval sword, Brasilian Jujutsu, boxing, Thai boxing, Capoeira and Karate. He has also practiced a number of approaches to Yoga, is a keen freediver and a Crossfit Instructor.

Edward is currently resident in Paris. He teaches Bagua in classes and seminars with a range of foci, from practical self defence to meditation and personal development.

For more information about Bagua, essays, techniques, free stuff, seminars and online training visit

www.i-bagua.com

and like our facebook page http://www.facebook.com/pages/I-Bagua/239683522723226

I-BAGUA

Printed in Great Britain
by Amazon